First World War
and Army of Occupation
War Diary
France, Belgium and Germany

17 DIVISION
Divisional Troops
236 Machine Gun Company
1 July 1917 - 28 February 1918

WO95/1995/3

The Naval & Military Press Ltd
www.nmarchive.com
Published in association with The National Archives

Published by

The Naval & Military Press Ltd

Unit 10 Ridgewood Industrial Park,

Uckfield, East Sussex,

TN22 5QE England

Tel: +44 (0) 1825 749494

www.naval-military-press.com

www.nmarchive.com

This diary has been reprinted in facsimile from the original. Any imperfections are inevitably reproduced and the quality may fall short of modern type and cartographic standards.

© Crown Copyright
Images reproduced by permission of The National Archives, London, England, 2015.

Contents

Document type	Place/Title	Date From	Date To
Heading	WO95/1995/3		
Heading	17 Div Troops 236 Machine Gun Company 1917 July-1918 Feb		
Heading	War Diary of 236 Machine Gun Company From 1st July 1917 to 31st July 1917 Volume 1		
War Diary	Belton Park Grantham	01/07/1917	15/07/1917
Miscellaneous			
War Diary	Arras	22/07/1917	31/07/1917
Heading	War Diary of 236 Machine Gun Company From 1st Augt 1917 to 31 Augt 1917 Volume 2		
War Diary	Arras	01/08/1917	17/08/1917
War Diary	Roclincourt Valley	18/08/1917	31/08/1917
Heading	War Diary of 236 Machine Gun Company From 1st Sept to 30th Sept 1917 Volume 3		
War Diary	Roclincourt Valley Arras	01/09/1917	12/09/1917
War Diary	Roclincourt Valley	13/09/1917	24/09/1917
War Diary	Simencourt	25/09/1917	26/09/1917
War Diary	Bouquemaison	27/09/1917	30/09/1917
Heading	War Diary of 236 Machine Gun Company From 1 Oct 17 to 31 Oct 17 Vol 4		
War Diary	Bouquemaison	01/10/1917	07/10/1917
War Diary	Proven	08/10/1917	10/10/1917
War Diary	In The March	10/10/1917	13/10/1917
War Diary	Langemark	14/10/1917	19/10/1917
War Diary	Proven	20/10/1917	21/10/1917
War Diary	Crasse Payelle	22/10/1917	29/10/1917
Miscellaneous			
Heading	War Diary of 236 Machine Gun Company From 18 November 1917 To 30th November 1917 Vol 5		
War Diary	Grasse Payelle	01/11/1917	01/11/1917
War Diary	Pas-de Calais	02/11/1917	05/11/1917
War Diary	Grasse Payelle Pas-De-Calais	06/11/1917	06/11/1917
War Diary	Langemarck Area	07/11/1917	07/11/1917
War Diary	Grasse-Payelle	07/11/1917	07/11/1917
War Diary	Friedland Camp	07/11/1917	17/11/1917
War Diary	Solferino Camp	20/11/1917	30/11/1917
Heading	War Diary of 236 Machine Gun Company From 1st to 31st December 1917 Vol 6		
War Diary	Langemarck Area (II) (Solferino Camp)	01/12/1917	05/12/1917
War Diary	Solferino Camp	06/12/1917	07/12/1917
War Diary	Pigeon Camp Proven	08/12/1917	09/12/1917
War Diary	Grasse Payelle	10/12/1917	11/12/1917
War Diary	Hillebrouck	12/12/1917	20/12/1917
War Diary	Beaulencourt	21/12/1917	22/12/1917
War Diary	Royaulcourt	23/12/1917	27/12/1917
War Diary	Trenches	28/12/1917	31/12/1917
Heading	War Diary of 236 Machine Gun Company From 1st January 1918 to 31st January 1918 Vol 7		
War Diary	Ruyaulcourt	01/01/1918	04/01/1918
War Diary	Line	05/01/1918	17/01/1918

War Diary	Line Havrincourt Hermies	17/01/1918	31/01/1918
Miscellaneous			
War Diary	Havrincourt	01/02/1918	28/02/1918

17 DIV TROOPS

236 MACHINE GUN COMPANY

1917 JULY - 1918 FEB

Army Form C. 2118.

WAR DIARY
or
INTELLIGENCE SUMMARY.
(Erase heading not required.)

Vol I

CONFIDENTIAL

War Diary
of
236 Machine Gun Company

From 1st July 1917 to 31st July 1917

(Volume 1)

WAR DIARY
or
INTELLIGENCE SUMMARY.

(Erase heading not required.)

Army Form C. 2118.

Place	Date	Hour	Summary of Events and Information	Remarks and references to Appendices
Bulton Park Grantown	1st to 12 July		Completed training - under orders to proceed overseas	S23
	12 July		Left camp 9.45 pm for Reading station en route to B.E.F. France - entrain without any casualties in spite of many M.G. Staff Officers.	S23
	13 July		Arrived Southampton 9 am. Company embarked on S.S. "HUNTSCRAFT" one hour , two motor/cycles to have into inspection substitutes provided. Steamer sailed 5.45 pm weather fine sea smooth	S23
	14 July		Arrived Havre about 8.30 am completed unloading 12.30 pm when company marched about three miles to I.A. Rest Camp.	S23
	15 July		Sunday spent day cleaning up & seeing Ordnance people in making up shortages in machine gun equipment. In the evening got orders to entrain on the following evening	S23

WAR DIARY
INTELLIGENCE SUMMARY

(Erase heading not required)

WAR DIARY
or
INTELLIGENCE SUMMARY.
(Erase heading not required.)

Army Form C. 2118.

Place	Date	Hour	Summary of Events and Information	Remarks and references to Appendices
ARRAS	22 July		Eight to ten German shells landed in or near vicinity of our camp	SS
"	23		G.O.C. Division inspected company two transport A & D sections pro into the trenches attached to 50 & 51 Companies for instruction, 2 OR to a gun Section of trenches in front of FAMPOUX	SS
"	24		Moved from ST NICHOLAS to camp in ROCLINCOURT valley	SS
"	25		Majority of Company employed erecting Nissen hut workshops etc	SS
"	26		training – Williams C. sevenly wounded also later.	SS
"	27		B.O.C. Sections relieve A.O.D	SS
"	28		training	SS

WAR DIARY
or
INTELLIGENCE SUMMARY.

(Erase heading not required.)

Army Form C. 2118.

Place	Date	Hour	Summary of Events and Information	Remarks and references to Appendices
ARRAS	29 July		Sunday Thunderstorms all day little work done	823
"	30th		3 guns of 4 Section relieve 3 anti aircraft positions manned by 30 Company.	824
"	31st		Mr Tate (now Sgt) now took over guns positions in the line B. section front guns D Section Mr Allen in command of D section as Mr Humphries is sick.	823

Signed R.S. Kinsey Capt
OC 236 Coy.

Army Form C. 2118.

WAR DIARY
or
INTELLIGENCE SUMMARY.
(Erase heading not required.)

Vol 2

CONFIDENTIAL

War DIARY

OF

236 MACHINE GUN COMPANY

FROM 1st AUGT 1917 TO 31 AUGT 1917

VOLUME 2

WAR DIARY
or
INTELLIGENCE SUMMARY.
(Erase heading not required.)

Army Form C. 2118.

Place	Date	Hour	Summary of Events and Information	Remarks and references to Appendices
ARRAS	1st		A Section 3 guns on A.A. went at Argou & Leavy dumps D. report sector B. left sector	&c
"	2		A Section relieved from A.A. positions by 175 M.G. Coy who came up from Somme district when they said were very quiet	&c
"	3		A Section under Mc Pain relieved B section, Mc Allen very quiet on this front	&c
"	4		Nothing particular during two weeks. Thunder	&c
"	6		C section relieves D section — a good deal too trim there in both sectors to make sections in the line even comfortable	&c
"	7		Two men Mouly & Barnett of C section passed by 9.20 shells which are fully unceasingly raid by the Boche — Barnett was pretty ill.	&c
"	9		B section relieves A. 2 reinforcements arrive from the Base — weather remains bad.	&c

WAR DIARY
or
INTELLIGENCE SUMMARY.
(Erase heading not required.)

Army Form C. 2118.

Place	Date	Hour	Summary of Events and Information	Remarks and references to Appendices
	10-11-12	evens	Nothing in particular doing. Capt Murray ill in bed	S43
	13	"	D returns C. section in left sector - Officers in left sector complains bitterly of staff offices in going away two gun positions by approaching them down the Town.	S43
	13a		A section relieves B in left sector. much fighting going on a few miles north opposite Lens.	S43
	16		Capt 2 men reinforcements arrive from the Base 1 section bombarded with gas shells no casualties	S43
	17		Mr Pain ill & is returned in the evening by Capt Simpson	S43

WAR DIARY
or
INTELLIGENCE SUMMARY.

Army Form C. 2118.

(Erase heading not required.)

Place	Date	Hour	Summary of Events and Information	Remarks and references to Appendices
ROCLINCOURT VALLEY	18 Aug		D Section in right sector are heavily bombarded all day. One gun & 4 men buried. Pte Shimo & Goulston go to hospital. Spare gun sent down in the evening	SU3
	19 Aug		Gun buried on 18th August little damage done to it	SU3
	20		B Section relieves A Section in left sector. C " " D " " right sector	SU3
	22		Weather continues to be very bad indeed. Amplifications at ANZIN Dump blown over 2 guns.	SU3
	23		Mr Allen returns. Capt Sampson — things are abnormally quiet on this front. There are expectations of the enemy retiring to DROCOURT QUEANT line which appears to be a strong one	SU3
	24		B Section relieved by A in left sector	SU3
	26		C " " D " right sector	

Army Form C. 2118.

WAR DIARY
or
INTELLIGENCE SUMMARY.
(Erase heading not required.)

Instructions regarding War Diaries and Intelligence Summaries are contained in F. S. Regs., Part II. and the Staff Manual respectively. Title pages will be prepared in manuscript.

Place	Date	Hour	Summary of Events and Information	Remarks and references to Appendices
ROCLINCOURT VALLEY	28 Augt		Pte Thorpe A section slightly accidentally wounded thro' carelessness in his own & Sergt Manning's tent. The Little finger injured by bullet – case of unloading motions not being correctly gone thro'. 2 Lieut Denny joins the company – first time in France – previous experience in Dardanelles	
	29		Mr Tam & McIlroy return Mr Allen in the left – weather still very bad.	
	30		Preliminary arrangements made with Divisional Company made with Divisions – very approximate. 7 van ferving allowance to remain in reserve camp. Turkish in many ways is a great one being well out for the side of a hill	
	31		Weather moreover very bad. Capt Sinton to Allen & Reeves got leave to go to Amiens for the day	

R.T. Kirby Captain,
No. 236 M.G. Coy., M.G.C.

A 5834 Wt. W4973/M687 750,000 8/16 D. D. & L. Ltd. Forms/C.2118/13.

WAR DIARY
or
INTELLIGENCE SUMMARY.

CONFIDENTIAL

WAR DIARY
of
236 Machine gun Company

From 1st Sept to 30th Sept 1917
(Volume 3)

WAR DIARY or INTELLIGENCE SUMMARY

Army Form C. 2118.

Place	Date	Hour	Summary of Events and Information	Remarks and references to Appendices
POELINCOURT VALLEY ARRAS	1 Sept		B. o. C. returns relieve A o D respectively in left & right sectors — Mr. McGregor relieves Mr. Humphries — Mr. Penn & Darby remain in the left. Things quiet in this sector — which rung down to improve the trenches. Organ are gone relieved by us in brigade.	see
	2 Sept		Decide to build statles & present camp with preparations for winter	see
	3 Sept		O.C. 2:0 51 Company dine at our mess	see
	4 Sept		Capt Simpson relieves Messrs Penn & Darby	see
	5 Sept		Nothing particular — DMGO's approvers stop felled to overhanging DMGO let present Major Poet of Black Watch	see
	6 Sept		Company at rest two sections out of the line just on route march to Maresuil — great improvements in the weather recently	see
	7 Sept		A o D returns relieve B o C respectively, 2 Lieut Penn gone to the left rest station suffering from Munro's Rheumatism	see
	8 Sept		Mr Allen appointed section commander of a section but him has been evacuated to Engelot. Everything normal, very quiet in the line — very little work from wiring in the way of improvements in the trenches being carried out.	see
	9/9/17			see

Army Form C. 2118.

WAR DIARY
or
INTELLIGENCE SUMMARY.
(Erase heading not required.)

Instructions regarding War Diaries and Intelligence Summaries are contained in F. S. Regs., Part II. and the Staff Manual respectively. Title pages will be prepared in manuscript.

Place	Date	Hour	Summary of Events and Information	Remarks and references to Appendices
Bouchavesnes Valley	13 Sept		B. & C. sections relieve A & D sections. We are making use of light railway & motor lorries for relief & returns in night trains.	SS3
	14 Sept		15 chinamen replace H.A. drivers on our right. We take over two A.A. guns at Argen Dump, Mr Klerry in charge.	SS3
	16 Sept		Lieut 18g P McElroy Sligt Carpar proceed to Corps Infantry school at HAUTES AVESNES	SS3
	18 Sept		Very successful raid by Manchesters, we shot a lot of Punchmet fire near VJ Salient. 205 M.G officer at A.O.D returns relieve B.O.C	SS3
	19 Sept		First intimation about the division moving out to rest	SS3
	20		Our guns all relieved on the evening as of	SS3
	20		a.a. guns	SS3
	23		Preparing to move	SS3
	24		Relieved by 61st division, handed over camp to DCLI Divver battalion. Company moved at 10.45am to SIMENCOURT into billets. We are for the most attached to the 37st Brigade.	SS4

WAR DIARY
or
INTELLIGENCE SUMMARY.

Army Form C. 2118.

Place	Date	Hour	Summary of Events and Information	Remarks and references to Appendices
SIMENCOURT	25 Sept		Many men suffering from effects of previous days march which was done at one half in a very hot sun with full kit & full kit cleaned up during morning. Free entertainment football matches in the afternoon.	443
	26 Sept		Got orders that we were attached to 52 Brigade for training — that we were move to BOUQUEMAISON indicated today — starting at 10 am we do a very good march of 17 miles we never fell out — we got very good billets in BOUQUEMAISON quite a clean village there under from DOULLENS.	443
BOUQUEMAISON	27 Sept		Start training	443
"	28 Sept		Started a Company Canteen in the Cinema as there is no other source for the Company buying is another its govern.	443
"	29 Sept		A section did practice attack with Manchester last Kents	443
"	30		Brigade night operations Church Parade pm	443

W.P. [signature] Captain,
Comdg. No. 236 M.G. Coy., M.G.C.

Army Form C. 2118.

WAR DIARY
or
INTELLIGENCE SUMMARY.
(Erase heading not required.)

Vol 4

CONFIDENTIAL

WAR DIARY

OF

236 MACHINE GUN COMPANY

from

1 Oct 17 to 31 Oct 17

Army Form C. 2118.

WAR DIARY
or
INTELLIGENCE SUMMARY.
(Erase heading not required.)

Instructions regarding War Diaries and Intelligence Summaries are contained in F. S. Regs., Part II. and the Staff Manual respectively. Title pages will be prepared in manuscript.

Place	Date	Hour	Summary of Events and Information	Remarks and references to Appendices
BOUQUEMAISON	1 Oct		Carried on with training – B.O.C. returns did testical others with Battalions	SM/
	2 Oct		Continue of training of 52 Brigade at LA SOUICH	SM/
	3 Oct		Prepared to move north – being getting prepared for entraining	SM/
	4 Oct		Marched to MONDICOURT entraining there at 1.42 pm entraining took successful arrived at PROVEN	SM/
	5 Oct		12.30 am marched into POMPEY CAMP which was in a very wet state. No casualties to men or animals on the journey.	SM/
	6 Oct		Cleaned up & prepare for going to line – played RAMC at football and 2nd very good game result 4 all – RAMC claimed to be best team in the division	SM/
	7 Oct		32 O.R's attached to no 1 erm infantry each battalion in division was represented but they were not at all a good lot – the sick never went returned & influenced by another rise.	SM/

WAR DIARY
or
INTELLIGENCE SUMMARY.
(Erase heading not required.)

Army Form C. 2118.

Place	Date	Hour	Summary of Events and Information	Remarks and references to Appendices
PROVEN	8th Oct		Training as usual. Capt. Gordon of 2nd Leinstery called on us 2 listed N.S. mills serves as a reinforcement.	S.03
	9 Oct		Training — Adm.O's conference with O.C. companies. Got orders to proceed next day to COPPERNOBLE camp 7am next day.	S.03
	10 Oct		Received orders move 2 am to proceed to trenches meeting guides at BOESINGHE at 1 km – entrance PROVEN to ELVERDINGHE where we had 2 hours wait on transport which came by road – on its arrival we set out for BOESINGHE where guides met us & proceeded towards LANGEMARK – had great trouble with trains in mud & ditches. Track's with congestion of traffic. Company proceeded to Pheasaenne N.E. of LANGEMARK by 18.9 LANGEMARK STATION took over from 58 & 127 companies who handed over badly but left us a good supply of ammn.	S.04

WAR DIARY or INTELLIGENCE SUMMARY

Place	Date	Hour	Summary of Events and Information	Remarks and references to Appendices
On the move	10 Oct		Transport 40 x.x.0 & C9NS returned to COPPERNOLLE CAMP reaching there 10 pm	SW
	11 Oct		Heavily shelled by the enemy but things nyt & proposed for following days attack	SW
	12 Oct		3rd Bgade attacked at dawn along with Guards Div on the Lft - Division suffered 1000 yds with slight casualties over 12 barrage guns put up a creditable show & were congratulated by G.S.O.1 - C section in reserve at LANGEMARK station advanced to support Nutts & Linty's were badly cut up by shell fire	SW
	13 Oct		S.O.S. went up 1 am & barrage played havoc with enemy forces massing for counter attack by the railway embankment. Weather very wet seen in shell holes having a very rough time	SW

WAR DIARY
or
INTELLIGENCE SUMMARY.
(Erase heading not required.)

Army Form C. 2118.

Place	Date	Hour	Summary of Events and Information	Remarks and references to Appendices
LANGEMARK	14		All returns sent under Pack animals - two mules killed one sinking in mud & having to be shot all 10 guns still in the line - weather very wet	SS3
	15		2 section badly cut up one sent out of the line also 2 Lieut Pearce & 2 Lieut Mills - other returns men are on tonnage work.	SS3
	16		Nothing of note happened -	SS3
	17		Transport & CQMS & details move back to PROVEN by train. to POMPEY CAMP - all company guns withdrawn from the line. Lieut McKay returns from leave apenty restored	SS3
	18		Sections from trenches arrive in the early morning day spent tending out shortages. Casualties during time 7 killed (including Sergt Tufs & Rodney) 18 wounded Lieut & 18 uncounced comes as a reinforcement.	SS3
	19		Cleaning up all day - inspection of MG officers held by Capt Linsey a/o/m GO in place of Major Hair yet gazetted	SS3

WAR DIARY
or
INTELLIGENCE SUMMARY.
(Erase heading not required.)

Army Form C. 2118.

Place	Date	Hour	Summary of Events and Information	Remarks and references to Appendices
PROVEN	20		Got orders to proceed troops to rest next day. Transport marches off at 7am	SA3
	21		Company goes by motor Lorries to GRASSE PAYELLE situated ½ way between Calais & St Omer.	SA3
GRASSE PAYELLE	22		O.C. Company off duty with bad burn result of mustard gas (a)	SA3
	23		Start training two batteries of Lewis guns for movement, barrage duties	SA3
	24		Carry on with training	SA3
	25		do	SA3
	26		do	SA3
	27		do	SA3
	28		do	SA3
	29		His tactical scheme with 50th Brigade, not a great success Major Colvin arrives as DMGO - Capt Knorey goes to Hospital 3 Military Medals awarded to Company.	SA3

WAR DIARY

INTELLIGENCE SUMMARY

(Erase heading not required.)

Instructions regarding War Diaries and Intelligence
Summaries are contained in F.S. Regs., Part II
and the Staff Manual respectively. Title pages
will be prepared in manuscript.

Army Form C. 2118.

WAR DIARY
or
INTELLIGENCE SUMMARY.

(Erase heading not required.)

Vol 5

CONFIDENTIAL.

WAR DIARY

OF

236 MACHINE GUN COMPANY.

FROM 1st NOVEMBER 1917

To 30th NOVEMBER 1917

WAR DIARY or INTELLIGENCE SUMMARY

Army Form C. 2118.

Place	Date	Hour	Summary of Events and Information	Remarks and references to Appendices
GRASSE-PAYELLE	1/1/17		During this period the company remained in training at GRASSE-PAYELLE. The company was reorganised into two batteries of six guns each, four guns of C section heavy attached to them six guns of A section, the battery being known as D battery under the command of Lieut McIlroy. The other battery E battery was composed of the four guns of D section with the two remaining guns of A section under the command of Lieut Underwood.	W.D.
PAS-DE-CALAIS	2/1/17			
	3/1/17		Attached to 236 M.G. Coy. also were six guns each of 50th M.G. Coy 51st M.G. Coy and 52nd M.G. Coy. The battery of 50 Coy was named A battery under the command of Lieut Irwin and 2/Lieut Culverwell, 51st Coy "B" battery in charge of 2/Lieut Rempel & 2/Lieut Higgins and the six guns of 52nd Coy C battery under 2/Lieut Ralph. These attached guns of the brigade	
	4/1/17			
	5/1/17		companies were attached to 236 Coy for rations the five batteries coming directly under the D.M.G.O. for administrative purposes	

Army Form C. 2118.

WAR DIARY
or
INTELLIGENCE SUMMARY.
(Erase heading not required.)

(2)

Place	Date	Hour	Summary of Events and Information	Remarks and references to Appendices
GRASSE-PAYELLE	6/11/17	A.M. 7.15	D. Battery and two guns of B section proceeded to AUDRUICQ and entrained for ELVERDINGHE at 9.0 A.M.	JMPM
PAS-DE-CALAIS.			Having reached their destination at 1.30 P.M. they marched to billets at MARSOUIN CAMP on the PILKEM RIDGE	
	7/11/17	A.M. 11.0	D Battery relieved a battery of 57th Divisional M.G. Coy.	
LANGEMARCK AREA			at OLGA HOUSES (1000ˣ S.E. LANGEMARCK & 400ˣ S. of YPRES - STADEN Railway) Company H.Q. being situated at DROP HOUSES (a "pill-box" centre of LANGEMARCK) where the two guns of B section were mounted for anti-aircraft duties.	JMPM
GRASSE-PAYELLE		A.M. 4.15	The remainder of the company paraded & moved to AUDRUICQ where they entrained for ELVERDINGHS & marched to FRIEDLAND CAMP (1000ˣ S. of YSER CANAL in the LANGEMARCQ area)	JMPM
			REF. 17ᵗʰ DIV. R.O. Nov 8ᵗʰ 1917.	
FRIEDLAND CAMP			Under Authority granted by H.M. the King the F.M. Comdg-in-Chief has awarded the following decoration The Military Cross 7/2/Lieut W.P. Allen 236 M.G. Coy the Army Corps & Divisional Commanders contratulate the recipient on gaining this award for gallantry.	JMPM

WAR DIARY
or
INTELLIGENCE SUMMARY

Army Form C. 2118.

(3)

Place	Date	Hour	Summary of Events and Information	Remarks and references to Appendices
FRIEDLAND CAMP	7/11		The award of the M.C. to 2/Lieut W.R. Allen M.C.	W.P.M.
			This decoration was awarded the above officer for gallantry in command of a machine gun battery in face of heavy hostile artillery fire. On Oct. 12th the 51st Bde. made a successful attack and on the following day the enemy made a strong counter attack astride the YPRES–STADEN railway. This attack was broken up with heavy casualties by our machine gun & artillery fire. The testimony of German prisoners to the effect that our machine gun fire was absolutely irresistible immediately north of the railway (where this Lewis gun barrage came down) proved the efficiency of the fire of the guns under this officers control. Considering extremely difficult conditions & casualties was nothing but extraordinary throughout. This officer's example of courage & endurance into the men under his command.	
			His conspicuous bravery and devotion to duty	22316 Sgt Peet H.E.
			had him awarded by Divisional Commander	82248 L/Sgt CROOK G.
			during this period the undermentioned	103570P 4/Sgt MORLEY G.E.
FRIEDLAND CAMP	6/11 to 15/11		relief took place regularly every four days to events of special importance occurred & casualties were slight being mainly in the approaches to and from the line	W.P.M.

WAR DIARY
or
INTELLIGENCE SUMMARY.

(Erase heading not required.)

Army Form C. 2118.

Place	Date	Hour	Summary of Events and Information	Remarks and references to Appendices
FRIEDLAND CAMP	17/11/17		The company moved from FRIEDLAND CAMP to SOLFERINO CAMP a matter of 500x further away from the YSER CANAL and adjoining DAWSONS CORNER to slightly drier and more comfortable conditions.	W.F.
SOLFERINO CAMP.	20/11/17		Command of the company was assumed on this date by Capt R.G. KINSEY (sick) in place of Capt W. FRANKLIN	W.F.
"	22/11/17		Orders were received at 1.30 p.m. to send two gun teams the hole immediately in lieu of an expected German offensive. 2/Lt T.W. Pearce set out accordingly at 3.15 p.m. to reconnoitre the positions to be adopted. The teams following at	
"	23/11/17		Reliefs took place of "C" & "A" batteries by "B" battery under 2/Lt W. Higgins & "E" battery under 2/Lt C.J. Devey & S. Leeton. Capt W. Franklin taking over from Lt D. Huw at DROP HOUSE - ?	W.F.
"	25/11/17		"E" battery located at FERDAN HOUSE was relieved from its to four guns two teams under 2/Lt C.J. Devey, representing these positions & turning the command of the battery under 2/Lt J. Leeton.	W.F.

WAR DIARY or INTELLIGENCE SUMMARY

Army Form C. 2118.

Place	Date	Hour	Summary of Events and Information	Remarks and references to Appendices
SOLFERINO CAMP	26/11/17		At the time of arrival in SOLFERINO CAMP the NE. O.S & men of the Bty. were all accommodated in tents. The brethern of Maxim guns at Mess Tackies was hand by D.O.R.E's. Good accommodation for all was provided by the 28th inst. Civilians were also cooks & gun Jemdars made with stables.	MPV
"	27/11/17		The guns were sent into the line under 2/Lt Bevis were covering our troops in the DEFENSIVE LINE. One of them were found unnecessary & guns were returned & left camp on this date.	MPV
"	28/11/17		As the remaining three guns were taken over by 52 Ind Bde in the afternoon of 28th when the following got which also took place: 2 L.G. Maxim & four guns of 2/Lt S Leith & remaining from guns of E Battery at FERDAN HOUSE in advance. 2/Lt Roeple & "C" battery relieved "B" battery at BEGA HOUSES. One gun team was also sent to relieve the gun in the DEFENSIVE LINE and manned by this day.	MPV
"	29/11/17		Reference is made in the 7th para to two guns intended for A.A. defence. These guns and remaining ammunition for destruction of continuing eqpt. In the enemy were handed to infantry.	MPV

Army Form C. 2118.

WAR DIARY
or
INTELLIGENCE SUMMARY.
(Erase heading not required.)

Place	Date	Hour	Summary of Events and Information	Remarks and references to Appendices
SOLFERINO CAMP	29/11/17 (contd.)		Reports: The teams have been robustly practicing with the battery rifle & are intending to put their shooting the morale. Three officers & the N.C.O's have attended several visual courses in the use of A.A. sights at the Hqrs of the 9th Squadron R.F.C. PROVEN. Average strength (infantry) of the day, both reserves, batteries has been during the past month — 17 officers 365 O.R. Three guns put out of action were taking over on 7th inst. Drawings supplies able on two lorries. Three guns were withdrawn.	Nos
"	30/11/17			Nos

[signature] Captain,
Comdg. No. 236 M.G. Coy., M.G.C.

[stamp: ORDERLY ROOM * No. 236 M.G. COY. M.G.C.]

Army Form C. 2118.

WAR DIARY
or
INTELLIGENCE SUMMARY.
(Erase heading not required.)

Vol 6

CONFIDENTIAL

WAR DIARY

of

236 MACHINE GUN COMPANY

FROM

1st to 31st DECEMBER 1917

Army Form C. 2118.

WAR DIARY
or
INTELLIGENCE SUMMARY.
(Erase heading not required.)

Instructions regarding War Diaries and Intelligence Summaries are contained in F.S. Regs., Part II. and the Staff Manual respectively. Title pages will be prepared in manuscript.

Place	Date	Hour	Summary of Events and Information	Remarks and references to Appendices
LANGEMARCK AREA (III)	1/12/17		Company (+ A B C batteries attacked) remained in the Langemarck area, two batteries being in the line at a time. C + D batteries were in the line from 1st to 4th inst.	JFPM
(SOLFERINO CAMP)	2/12/17		Training + camp improvement. A quiet time in the line.	JFPM
	3/12/17		2/Lt Turner + A battery relieved 2/Lt Raffle + C section. 2/Lt Dewey + E battery relieved 2/Lt Mills + D battery.	JFPM
	4/12/17		Training in camp. Baths for the men relieved from the line. The weather began to harden, with heavy frosts at night.	JFPM
	5/12/17		A quiet day in the line. An unfortunate accident occurred in camp to-day. At 5.30 P.M. the alarm was given that hostile aircraft were in the vicinity + shortly afterwards 5 bombs were dropped on SOLFERINO CAMP. One bomb fell on the transport hut with disastrous effect. Casualties 8 men killed 3 died of wounds 23 wounded. Fortunately the 52nd Field Ambulance was situated within 150x + the wounded men were rapidly transferred there to attended to. Two horses + three mules were wounded at the same time.	JFPM

WAR DIARY
or
INTELLIGENCE SUMMARY.
(Erase heading not required.)

Army Form C. 2118.

Place	Date	Hour	Summary of Events and Information	Remarks and references to Appendices
SOLFERINO CAMP	6/12/17		During the morning the men in camp were employed in cleaning up the camp after last night's disaster. Volunteers were called for from the company with any experience of horse management which met with a good response, the sufficient number being obtained to complete the transport.	JFMcK
	7/12/17	11.0 AM	The Senior Chaplain (C of E) 17th Division held a burial service at SOLFERINO Cemetery for the men killed last night at which representatives from all sections of the company were present.	
		8.15 AM	The company paraded & marched off at 8.30 to PIGEON CAMP CANADA area PROVEN. The men were all under canvas & it was rather cold but fine.	JFMcK
PIGEON CAMP	8/12/17		A full mornings training followed by football in the afternoon. At this period the company was very much employed in moving to so many men of the section being employed with the transport. A severe test for the new transport drivers which they passed with every credit.	JFMcK
PROVEN				
	9/12/17	9.0 PM	Entrained at PROVEN Station for GRASSE PAYELLE, LIGOUES AREA.	WFMcK

Army Form C. 2118.

WAR DIARY
or
INTELLIGENCE SUMMARY.
(Erase heading not required.)

Instructions regarding War Diaries and Intelligence Summaries are contained in F. S. Regs., Part II. and the Staff Manual respectively. Title pages will be prepared in manuscript.

Place	Date	Hour	Summary of Events and Information	Remarks and references to Appendices
GRASSE PAYELLE	10th Dec		Arrived in early hours of the morning from PROVEN. Uphill some billets as on October day spent resting. Having a settling down – 50th MG Company billets returned to their own company.	2/3
	11th		Company moved at 9am by road to HILLEBROUCK a small village in EPERLECQUES AREA return billets are good – Officers mainly portion of Chateau owned by an Englishman – very hospitable, trifle. Days march approximately 8 miles.	3/3
HILLEBROUCK	12		Good hard weather – a full morning's training, short spell to men trained ushers are required to replace as are now dangerously near trusting point.	3/3
	13		Another Coys training with A.V.D action football match in the afternoon. A score 5 to 2 goals. H.Q action properly established with CSM as Skilism	3/3

Warren Butler

WAR DIARY
or
INTELLIGENCE SUMMARY.
(Erase heading not required.)

Army Form C. 2118.

Place	Date	Hour	Summary of Events and Information	Remarks and references to Appendices
HILLERMUIR	14th		Draft of 30 men arrived yesterday, not a very good draft. Company mess with Pioneers to third army	
	15		entrain at ARQUES near ST OMER at 11.30 pm. detrain at ACHIET MIRAUMONT about 11am & march to camp at ACHIET LE GRAND - Snow & hard frost - morning very cold.	SU3
	16		Very cold, snowing - therecom to move in lorry Banne	SU3
	17		Very cold, snowing still Snow & frost	SU3
	18		Company move at 9.45 am by road ore BAPAUME to a small unfortable place called BEAULEN COURT - own midst 50th Brigade	SU3
	19		Extremely wld in enclosed gardens Magen Huts & civilian amount of snowing there	SU3
	20		Still bitterly cold - 2 Cant Lieut to posted as sub section officers to B Section	SU3

Army Form C. 2118.

WAR DIARY
or
INTELLIGENCE SUMMARY.
(Erase heading not required.)

Place	Date	Hour	Summary of Events and Information	Remarks and references to Appendices
BEAUCAMP	21		Fine with training – OC o 2 i/c reconnoitre line	See 3
	22		HAVRINCOURT sector. Training & camp improvements. Coys to move to ROYAULCOURT by road with one company to go on advance. Reconnre – 52 Brigade on right 53 Brigade on left.	See 3
ROYAULCOURT	23		Training – Lively night with aeroplane bombs on men. Killed one, wounded 6. Another billet badly damaged.	See 3
	24		Training – weather still hard & cold.	See 3
	25		£20 out of comforts fund provided men with plenty groceries.	See 3
	26		Training	See 3
	27		"	See 3
TRENCHES	28		The trenches relieve 51 M.G Coy on left sector – very rough conditions going in – arrangements only quite satisfactory	See 3
	29		Quiet day in the line	See 3
	30		Heavy shells between 7 & 8am. Left Bank killed 4083 Warwick	See 3

WAR DIARY
or
INTELLIGENCE SUMMARY.

Army Form C. 2118.

Place	Date	Hour	Summary of Events and Information	Remarks and references to Appendices
Izeaux	31 Dec		Last day attached to 52 MG Company. Company return to RUYAULCOURT — 2/Lt Thomson Lieut at O.C. 236 MG Company	

Army Form C. 2118.

WAR DIARY
or
INTELLIGENCE SUMMARY.
(Erase heading not required.)

96/7

Confidential

War Diary

of

236 Machine Gun Company

From 1st January 1918 to 31st January 1918

Army Form C. 2118.

WAR DIARY
or
INTELLIGENCE SUMMARY.
(Erase heading not required.)

Instructions regarding War Diaries and Intelligence Summaries are contained in F. S. Regs., Part II. and the Staff Manual respectively. Title pages will be prepared in manuscript.

Place	Date	Hour	Summary of Events and Information	Remarks and references to Appendices
RUAULCOURT	1 Jany 18		Cleaned up guns the after cleaning was carried on with thawing a.a. guns at YTRES firing.	SV3
"	2		Returns to YORKS & LANCS firing. BUS it	SV3
"	3		Got orders re spreading guns were took over of divisional front Mc Henry & another 0th sm gun reconnoitring work Transport & C.Q.M.S. move to VELU I company G.S. into	SV3
"	4		Aspinwar time 12 guns in H at Company H.Q. in Support - another four hard post, much enemy aeroplane activity - 2 Drivers & not to Rest	SV3
LINE	5		Ruse some of the gun positions which were of necessity hastily taken up - thrown more shells two Engcrs frontage in front of HERMES & HAVRINCOURT	SV3
	6,7,8,9,10		Little doing except work on dugouts & emplacements	SV3

WAR DIARY
or
INTELLIGENCE SUMMARY.
(Erase heading not required.)

Army Form C. 2118.

Place	Date	Hour	Summary of Events and Information	Remarks and references to Appendices
LINE	11/1/18		March wind up about possible Bosch attack - but nothing to come of it - Manchesters had over 30 posters of 90 men. Ivas a certain front.	
	12.13.14		Much swinging being done - much more care appears to taken with dispersion arrangements than previously. Capt Franklin returns from leave 13th up line 14th	
	15th		2 Lieut Allen M.C. one of Freddie's men returns from leave - turns out great - hopes of the war coming to an early conclusion.	
	16		A cold thaw sets in - mud trouble - trenches all falling in - little movement during day down in this front of the line.	
	17		Capt Young of DMGO catches Major Calder as our counter walks us - a disgrace of themes.	

Army Form C. 2118.

WAR DIARY
or
INTELLIGENCE SUMMARY.
(Erase heading not required.)

Instructions regarding War Diaries and Intelligence Summaries are contained in F. S. Regs., Part II. and the Staff Manual respectively. Title pages will be prepared in manuscript.

Place	Date	Hour	Summary of Events and Information	Remarks and references to Appendices
LINE HAZEBROUCK HERMIES	17.18		Company still run as in line with all guns in one battle positions	S.A.3
	19		A Section relieves D in CHARGES STREET C " " B in SPOIL HEAP relief done by daylight	S.A.3
	20.21		Transport Officer 2nd Lieut Kelly goes on leave to U.K. At time at present prove is via HAVRE there now instructions requests leave from this coin	S.A.3
	22		Sentor (B) Zwitten Dier (D) Robinson (c)	S.A.3
	23.30		Brenten on the front at Henry Close is 46 secants E.A. very active in front day B relieves C " D relieves A Extensive enemy B coming twenty against Capt Bergman C Force another trenches twenty against this company comes to view with this month.	S.A.3
	31st		26 days time in the line this month.	S.A.3

S.A. Whinman Lieut
for OC 236 M.G. Company

Forms/C/2118/4

Army Form C. 2118.

WAR DIARY
or
INTELLIGENCE SUMMARY.
(Erase heading not required.)

Instructions regarding War Diaries and Intelligence Summaries are contained in F. S. Regs., Part II. and the Staff Manual respectively. Title pages will be prepared in manuscript.

Place	Date	Hour	Summary of Events and Information	Remarks and references to Appendices

(A.883) Wt. W36/JM1672 350,000 4/17 D. D. & L., London, E.C. **Sch. 52a** Forms/C/2118/4

23rd MGBn Army Form C. 2118.

WAR DIARY
or
INTELLIGENCE SUMMARY.
(Erase heading not required.)

Place	Date	Hour	Summary of Events and Information	Remarks and references to Appendices
HAVRINCOURT	1.2.18		Companies still remain in the line with the 6th Division on	
			left & 47th Division on right.	
	2,3,4th		An exceptionally quiet time in this sector — nothing of	
			interest to report.	
	5,6,7th		The situation remains quiet. At night enemy aeroplanes	
			appear to take advantage of moonlight nights to be	
			constant source of bombing.	
			Situation unchanged	
	8,9,10th		G.H.Q. decide to re-organize the Machine Gun Corps and	
	11.18		to form a Divisional M.G. Bn. Major D.S. Callen to be put	
			D.M.G.O. is appointed to command the 17th Bn. M.G.C.	
			The new organization provides for Bn HQ consisting	
			of C.O. (Lt Col) Second in command (Major) Adjutant	
			Qn. M.O. Signalling Officer Transport Officer Reconnaissance	
			Companies — they are to be commanded by a Major with	
			a Captain as Second in command	

WAR DIARY
or
INTELLIGENCE SUMMARY.
(Erase heading not required.)

Army Form C. 2118.

Place	Date	Hour	Summary of Events and Information	Remarks and references to Appendices
HAVRINCOURT	13/6		HAVRINCOURT village inwards shelled	
	14-17/6		A very quiet week, nothing of interest to report. The Company are still remaining in this line and are engaged in consolidating them & also mopping up mines in Havrincourt in accordance with the divisional scheme of defence for this sector.	
	18.19/6		Very fine weather, enemy aeroplanes presenting much activity. Our battery takes advantage of this and visiblely to enemy aircraft, welcomes shots. Capt. Rinser MO (late of this company) is attached to HQ 17th Bn MGC.	
	20/6		Received in command of 17th Bn MGC	
	21/6		A party of 4 officers + 10 OR proceed on leave to UK	
	22/6		An advance party moved off in readiness to move to report 11th Division after the Bn. proceeds from MG June 24th Bk.M	
	27/6 28/6		15 NCOs + men proceed to UK on 14 days leave. Spasmodic shellfire was noticed during the night, chiefly by enemy ?gas? ?ammo? ?pits? with ??calibre? guns.	

www.ingramcontent.com/pod-product-compliance
Lightning Source LLC
Chambersburg PA
CBHW081456160426
43193CB00013B/2502